LETTS GUIDES TO
❖ GARDEN DESIGN ❖
Containers

LETTS GUIDES TO
✧ GARDEN DESIGN ✧

Containers

✧ PHILIP SWINDELLS ✧

CANOPY BOOKS
A Division of Abbeville Publishing Group

NEW YORK   LONDON   PARIS

First published in the United States in 1994
by Canopy Books, a division of Abbeville Publishing Group
488 Madison Avenue
New York NY 10022

First published in the United Kingdom in 1993
by Charles Letts & Co Ltd.
Letts of London House, Parkgate Road
London SW11 4NQ

Series editor: Diana Saville

Edited, designed and produced by Robert Ditchfield Ltd.
Copyright © Robert Ditchfield Ltd. 1993.

ISBN 1-55859-663-1

A CIP catalogue record for this book is available from the British Library.

ACKNOWLEDGMENTS

Photographs are reproduced by kind permission of the following: Pat Brindley: 18;
Robert Ditchfield Ltd.: 22, 52/53 (York Gate, photographer Jerry Hardman-Jones);
Lamontagne/Garden Picture Library: cover; Andrew Lawson: 24; W. A. Lord: 30/31;
S & O Matthews: 42, 43 (Chilcombe House); Clive Nichols: 48/49, 55 (both Fulham
garden, designer Anthony Noel); Christine Skelmersdale: 29; Stapeley Water
Gardens: 16/17; Thompson & Morgan: 37, 40. All other photographs are by
Diana Saville who would like to thank the owners of the gardens which include
Batemans (33), Barnsley House (14), Bourton House (1, 7, 12, 25, 32, 36, 38, 39,
41, 44, 60), Burford House (6, 13 right), Close Farm (20/21). Edenbridge House
(45, 47, 57), Hergest Croft (50), Hill Court (30, 51), Lower Hall (8), Lower Hope (10,
28, 48), Marley Bank (23 above), Oxford Botanic Gardens (23 below), Powis Castle
(13 left), Preen Manor (2, 15, 26, 27), Sissinghurst Castle (10/11), Snowshill (58),
Stone Cottage (59), Weston Hall (61), Woodlands (46), Woodpeckers (9).

ILLUSTRATIONS

Page 1: Pelargonium, echeverias and black-leafed ophiopogon.
Frontispiece: Delightful and idiosyncratic pot-garden.
Page 5: Planted wheelbarrow in a cottage garden.

CONTENTS

ABOVE: *Corner pots emphasize the formal pool.*
OPPOSITE: *A hooded frame for a large assembly of pelargoniums,* Argyranthemum frutescens *and the glaucous* Melianthus major.

INTRODUCTION

The cultivation of plants in containers is becoming increasingly popular. Modern materials have made the production of all manner of tubs, planters and baskets more economical than ever before, while scientifically formulated composts can guarantee success if simple cultural rules are followed. There is no longer any need to have large bulky urns and troughs that take two people to move, nor the struggle with a soil that is of inadequate structure. Add to this the modern trend to ever smaller gardens and one can readily appreciate why growing plants in containers has become so widespread.

For the gardener with only a small backyard or patio, tubs and planters offer the only real opportunity for introducing colour and interest. Such plants are not only good for the soul, but absolutely essential to take the harshness away from hard landscaped areas. Arranging containers in groups, or if the paving is pleasing, as focal points, can transform a dull hard area into one of beauty. While it is pleasant to have luxuriant foliage everywhere, sometimes a more restful effect can be achieved by the strategic placement of two tubs containing well clipped shrubs.

It is the mobility of containers that is their greatest virtue. If a particular arrangement is not pleasing it is easily changed. Fair-weather gardeners can decide only to garden during the summer and abandon the planters to the garage or potting-shed for the winter. Winter gardening need consist of no more than sweeping the patio.

For the enthusiast the container, whether it be tub or basket, provides a great opportunity for making an intensive floral picture. The gardener is pitting his wits against nature and yet it almost always comes off. It is staggering that gardeners should expect plants that are jammed into a tightly confined basket and hung in the air to prosper, for this is most unnatural behaviour. Yet the plants flourish and provide a feature that can be achieved by no other means.

This pushing of plants to their limit and

succeeding is largely the result of the development of modern composts, which in turn have made container gardening what it is today. Within the confines of a planter it is possible to create colour effects of a richness, diversity and intensity that are unattainable elsewhere in the garden. Plants can be packed closely together and providing they are carefully manicured and watched for diseases, they will fulfil their potential.

While this intensity of cultivation and spectacle of colour appeals to both the keen gardener and the householder with little but hard landscaping, it is also very welcome for those who find it increasingly difficult to bend. Carefully selected containers can be cultivated at a reasonable height; even hanging baskets can now be attached to simple pulleys for raising or lowering at will. For the elderly or infirm gardener, containers are the perfect answer.

Siting and Aspect

In theory there is no reason why plants in containers cannot be grown successfully, whatever the position. If carefully and tastefully planted with hardy ferns in a leafy soil-based compost, a tub or urn is capable of producing a picture of simple beauty in a damp, gloomy, shady corner. Few other plants would prosper here. However, a possible alternative might be a coloured-leafed hosta like *Hosta undulata mediovariegata*; or Solomon's seal, *Polygonatum multiflorum*, perhaps mixed with dwarf hardy maidenhair ferns, especially if grown together in a shallow stone trough.

Thus the careful selection of the plant for the position is the key to success. Whilst it is possible to put a container anywhere, it is what you put in it that matters. Of course, the type of compost used is also important, for

Wide steps are an ideal site for pots, as the display is spread over varying levels.

Planted troughs and staddle stones add interest to the rug of plants.

within the confines of a tub or basket the plants are more dependent than ever upon the gardener's skill in getting the growing medium right, and afterwards ensuring that it remains in good order.

Soil-based compost should be used for all permanent plantings. The soil content serves as a buffer against the potential problems of heavy feeding, an essential for most container-grown plants. These not only suffer confinement, but are often grown very close together. The regular feeding of soil-less composts leads to their rapid decline. Most will last a season, but after that their structure is in doubt. The effect of feeding upon the main component, which is often peat or bark, leads to its steady decomposition. What starts to appear in the container is a miniature compost heap which becomes steadily compacted and airless, ultimately to become the home of troublesome sciarid flies.

Soil-less composts are ideal for summer bedding plants, hanging baskets and other containers where the display is changed regularly. Soil-based composts should serve permanent plants, although there is no reason to deny their use for the summer show; it is just that plants are unlikely to attain maturity quite so quickly in a heavier colder medium.

Water is a vital ingredient for the successful cultivation of all plants in containers. Regular attention is a commitment that every gardener needs to make. However, much can be done to ensure that the minimum of watering is required. While sunny places lead to rapid drying-out they are also necessary for the well-being of many plants. The combination of sun and wind, though, is potentially devastating, so never site containers or hanging baskets where they have the additional hazard of drying by the wind.

Choose a place that is easily accessible. If a hanging basket is situated where a step ladder is needed every time it requires watering, then it is unlikely to be watered regularly. Tubs and containers placed in distant parts of the garden invite similar neglect, so when they are used as focal points, be sure that there is a regular and accessible supply of water. Ideally tubs and planters should be close to the house, where watering can become part of a simple routine.

CHOOSING A CONTAINER

There are really no restrictions upon the types of containers that can be used for growing plants. The only limitations are set by the gardener's imagination. Any container that has sufficient depth to take enough compost for the intended plants can be utilized, providing that it has some simple arrangement for drainage. Waterlogging is the most frequent factor in the failure of unconventional containers.

Garden centres are full of a whole range of elegant and decorative planters in materials as diverse as plastic and reconstituted stone. All can find a place in the garden. It is up to the individual to select something that is to his taste, but within this choice the well-being of the intended planting must figure highly, so container design is very important.

Any planter or window box must have a minimum depth of 6in/15cm if it is to allow for proper root development. A greater depth is more desirable. Bearing this in mind, carefully assess, before purchase, any urn or similar container with a shallow area around the rim. If the outer planting is unable to penetrate the main central body of compost, then, with constant drying out, the plants will be permanently stressed.

Drainage must also be provided, preferably by holes in the base of the planter or window box, although in containers without holes a generous layer of gravel in the bottom before soil or compost is added will work satisfactorily if watering is carefully attended to.

Containers that are to be used all the year round must also be frost-proof. Not only the materials from which they are made, but also to some extent the insulation that they can provide for the roots of plants. Thin-walled plastic tubs are light and easy to handle, but permit the easy passage of cold, while wooden tubs, although heavy and unwieldy, provide considerable insulation.

Along with drainage, resistance to extremes of temperature is vital for the success of year-round plantings. Plants that are ordinarily hardy in the open ground often succumb to root-kill in a container which freezes solidly during the winter. This also points to the provision of as large a container as possible for any plantings that are to remain outside all winter. The greater the volume of compost, the less likely that freezing is going to prove a problem.

The weight of a container can also be an important consideration. If a planting is going to be tall – which might well be the case with a shrub – then the container should be large enough to be stable when filled with compost. Leafy half-standard box or bay trees can easily be turned over in the wind if growing in a less than substantial planter.

On the other hand a lightweight material is desirable for window boxes or any other types of planters that are fixed to a wall. The lighter the material, the more weighty, substantial and generally better the compost can be.

ABOVE LEFT: *Tender Clivia miniata, its brilliant flowers toning well with its rust brown earthenware container.*

ABOVE: *An old copper, flanked by columnar yews, is the central focus of interest.*

Terracotta container, planted with diascia, Felicia amelloides and pink lobelia.

Terracotta, Stone, Wood

Planters and containers are manufactured in many different ways. For the traditional garden the warm browns of terracotta are the most appreciated. Not only are they more natural-looking than many other modern materials, but they have friendly associations with the past. Being of a neutral appearance they can accept almost any floral mixture or strong individual colour, and whether it is a subtle pink, pastel lavender or brilliant orange, the colours of both flowers and pot blend harmoniously.

Modern reconstituted stone confers similar benefits, but because of its more bulky and substantial nature it is less versatile. The range of plants that are suitable for the weighty stone container are considerably less

owing to the more specialized uses and positions of such ornaments.

The great benefit that reconstituted stone has over terracotta is its durability. Although manufacturers of terracotta pots often offer a frost-guarantee or claim frost-resistance, in reality there are no terracotta pots that can withstand protracted freezing in the same way as reconstituted stone. If choosing terracotta be aware of its possible limitations during winter when full of frozen compost.

The same applies to glazed pots. These should only be used where severe freezing is unlikely. Some are of a plain glaze which provides a natural foil for plants, but others are either etched or painted with patterns or motifs. These need to be carefully selected or they can detract from the plants. On the other hand they can become the feature themselves, the soft green lines of fern foliage complementing the beauty of the planter.

When purchasing a terracotta or glazed planter, select suitable feet as well. These are small movable supports upon which a container can be set in order to lift it off the ground. This permits the free passage of water through the drainage holes and also prevents the pot or planter from freezing to the ground, when there is a danger of terracotta shaling and flaking.

Wooden containers present no such problems. Resistant to frost and, if properly cured and treated, impervious to the rain, these are the most versatile containers of all, although they do not rest easily in all garden designs. The ones with a planed finish and simple carving are the most useful, especially the kind that has a detachable side through which the plant can be removed for repotting. These are based upon the design of the tubs

formerly used for growing citrus in orangeries and can be used in almost all situations.

Barrels and tubs, along with rough-hewn wooden planters, need a more rustic setting. These are excellent for permanent plantings. They are mostly larger than other containers and much more economical. While there are many different kinds available at garden centres, it is quite possible to build your own structure or else make a perfectly respectable tub out of an old barrel.

Plastic should not be neglected, for although the least pleasing to the eye it is very economical. It is light as well, and providing that it has adequate drainage usually makes an excellent practical home for plants. Look out for stone-coloured or grey tubs and pots rather than glaring whites. These discolour much more slowly than those with a white finish which by the end of the first season begin to look jaded.

Unpainted wooden box for fuchsia, Helichrysum petiolare *and* ageratum.

Artificial stone container, well sited on its small ivy-covered plinth.

TUBS AND BARRELS

Tubs and barrels can be used for a wide range of plantings, whether permanent or transitory, but they are predominantly used for shrubby or perennial plantings. Practically they are best suited to this kind of use, for permanent plants require solid and substantial containers. Visually their use for shrub or conifer cultivation is more appealing, for tubs and barrels are essentially a fairly heavy feature which can dominate a planting of spring or summer bedding.

That is not to say that such arrangements should be excluded, for if very carefully contrived they can be a success. However, in combination with a permanent planting they will be more appealing.

Shrubs and conifers of various kinds have long been inhabitants of tubs and barrels. They are structural and moveable parts of the garden scene which have become increasingly important in recent years with the greater use of hard landscaping materials for paths, patios and sitting-out areas. Indeed under many circumstances they are the only satisfactory method of softening harsh and glaring building materials.

They are also used as punctuation marks, making a very definite statement in predetermined parts of the

ABOVE: *The twin conifer cones will act as evergreen sculptures all the year.*

OPPOSITE: *Unpretentious half-barrel, comfortably clad by its staked pelargonium and trailing Helichrysum petiolare.*

garden landscape, perhaps to add symmetry to a formal water feature, or to create a focal point in a garden vista. With the limitations of space in the modern garden, container-cultivated woody plants can often successfully achieve an effect that is elusive when attempted with a permanent planting in open ground.

Not all shrubs and conifers are well suited to life in a tub or barrel, but most of the broad-leafed evergreens adapt well. These include camellias, aucuba, dwarf rhododendrons and Japanese azaleas. Deciduous shrubs such as the mollis azaleas, spiraeas like the bridal wreath (Spiraea 'Arguta'), and the shrubby potentillas are first-class tub plants. All produce good fibrous root systems that are a prerequisite for container growing.

Conifers with a more flattened fern-like foliage adapt to a restricted root run. These include the myriad cypress varieties as well as the western red cedars or thujas. Needle-bearing conifers such as the spruce and firs are not so easily managed as they are very susceptible to fluctuations in the soil's moisture content.

Providing that conifers and broad-leafed evergreens are kept well watered during the summer, they come to little harm. It is only in intensive heat that they are likely to show any signs of stress.

Evergreens that become frozen solid in their containers during the winter months, although very hardy, may die by the spring. The whole root system freezes, the plant is unable to take up water and dies, not of cold but drought.

15

Tiny water garden in a ceramic pot; the tender pale blue Eichhornia crassipes is on the right.

MINIATURE WATER GARDEN

Any small container that is capable of holding water can be used to create a miniature water garden. Old galvanized water tanks, sinks and baths with their outlets plugged are all extremely serviceable, especially if sunk in the ground. Metal containers may eventually corrode and leak unless protected initially with a good coat of rubber-based paint. Old wine and vinegar casks can be turned into excellent small pools when sawn in half, but tubs that may have contained oils, tar or wood preservative should be avoided as any residue that remains is likely to pollute the water, forming an unsightly scum on the surface.

Before planting a container, make sure that it is thoroughly cleaned. Use clear water, never detergent as it is difficult to be certain when all traces have been removed. As a couple of small fish are necessary in order to control mosquito larvae, untainted water is essential. With tanks or sinks where algae have become established, add enough potassium permanganate crystals to the water to turn it violet. With the aid of a stiff brush, any clinging algae are easily removed and no harmful residue will be left behind.

Once the container is clean, spread a 3in/7.5cm layer of good garden soil or aquatic planting compost over the floor. If garden soil is used be sure that it has not been recently dressed with artificial fertilizer as this will ensure the rapid development of green water-discolouring algae. Make the soil into a muddy consistency by adding a little water and the miniature water garden will be ready for planting.

Planting should ideally take place during spring, but can be continued into summer if necessary. Choose a miniature waterlily such as the canary yellow *Nymphaea* 'Pygmaea Helvola' or its white cousin *N.* 'Pygmaea Alba' as a centre-piece. Or perhaps the dwarf version of the yellow pond lily, *Nuphar minima*. Around the edge use the miniature reedmace, *Typha minima*, with its tiny brown poker heads, or the slender powder-blue flowered *Mimulus ringens*. Water

Wooden half-barrel allows a good depth of water for the miniature waterlilies.

forget-me-not, bog arum and water mint may also be tried, although the latter may need controlling towards the end of the season. A restrained submerged plant like hair grass, *Eleocharis acicularis* can complete the picture.

After planting and before water is added, cover the entire soil surface with a thin layer of well washed pea shingle to prevent fish from disturbing the soil in their quest for insect larvae. Take the end of the hosepipe that is to be used for filling the container and put it in a large polythene bag before placing on the floor of the container. This prevents disturbance of the compost as the water flows in. The bag is removed with the hosepipe when the required level has been reached.

Add a portion of a floating plant like frogbit, *Hydrocharis morsus-ranae*, half a dozen ramshorn snails and a couple of small goldfish and the watery world is complete. Routine maintenance consists of removing fading leaves and flower heads and regularly topping up with water. It is preferable to take the fish indoors for the winter months. Their survival is always in doubt in such a small volume of water.

Apart from using tubs and sinks for hardy aquatic plants, consider the possibilities offered by half-hardy aquatics. Some of the tropical waterlily varieties flourish in such a situation, together with the sacred lotus or nelumbo, and old favourites like the water hyacinth (*Eichhornia crassipes*) and water poppy (*Hydrocleys commersonii*).

A tall tower gives the effect of a cascade when assembled, as each planting pocket can hold its own plant. Although made of white plastic, the least attractive of all container materials, the plants – petunias, begonias and impatiens – soon cover it with their rapid growth.

PLANTERS AND TOWERS

Modern planters and towers are an acquired taste. They do not rest easily in a traditional informal garden, but they are a quite acceptable aspect of the modern home and garden. Planters come in all shapes and sizes; they are often reproductions of urns or tubs and usually made of modern synthetic materials. Their colours are not always engaging, but they can be rapidly disguised with foliage, for they are intended for plant cultivation and with modern soil-less composts mostly provide a very good environment for the plants.

Towers are not always so well designed, although recently great improvements have been witnessed. The best of these create a structure 5 – 6ft/1.5 – 1.8m tall, built with sectional pieces. The lower part is like a tub, often with a built-in self-watering device, and with a pocket for planting in each wall. Succeeding sections have no base and pockets in each wall. One section is added to another until they reach the desired height.

Each section is filled with compost as it is added, the best towers having a special tube that fits through the centre so that watering can be easily attended to. It is very difficult to keep a 5ft/1.5m high tower damp merely by watering it from the top. Planting takes place in the pockets as the tower is erected, the plants being pushed through the holes and firmed from within.

The opportunities offered by towers and modern planters are many, but they are restricted to plants of short duration. None are really suitable for permanent long-term plantings. Planters are best used for bedding subjects, both spring and summer: wallflowers and tulips, forget-me-nots and daisies as well as pansies in the spring, pelargoniums, fuchsias, marigolds and lobelia during summer. Towers can be used for cascading plants, but are often used most effectively for growing herbs or trouble-free strawberries.

A strawberry tower need not be boring, for the leaves of modern varieties, when regularly sprayed against fungal diseases, are not dis-pleasing and the great show of white spring blossoms is an absolute delight. The fruits are a welcome bonus, but need netting from hungry birds who find them despite the unconventional method of culture. All strawberries grow well in towers, but 'Bogota' and 'Hapil' are two well tried sorts, and if you are looking for decorative foliage, then the less pro-ductive *Fragaria ananassa* 'Variegata' has cream-and-green variegated leaves that are in character all summer long.

Towers can also be very effectively used for herbs. Parsley, pot marjoram and thyme all flourish under these conditions. The lovely blue-flowered hyssop and grey-leafed horehound are other welcome additions, along with both summer and winter savory. Avoid any of the cow parsley family such as dill, fennel, lovage and angelica. These are much too vigorous to contain.

Some bedding plants grow well in a tower structure.

Herb tower fashioned out of two layers of intermossed chicken-wire, lined with black plastic; it is filled with earth as the herbs are inserted through holes in the wire. These include chervil, parsley, thyme, sage, purple basil, hyssop and a scented-leafed pelargonium.

Pansies seem to find life very acceptable here. So too im-patiens of most kinds, except the New Guinea hybrids. Certainly the dwarfer 'Elfin' strains are very much at home. Petunias love growing in towers if you place them out of the wind, the beautiful double 'Blue Danube' in soft lavender-blue making a grace-ful display.

19

Stone trough of pansies and lobelia, admirably set so that it grows out of its surrounding plants

SINKS AND TROUGHS

While there are still opportunities for buying old stone sinks or troughs, they are very fashionable objects and likely to remain out of the financial reach of most home gar-

deners. They also have limitations, as few have adequate drainage and they can be difficult to adapt for the cultivation of plants. Old porcelain sinks are a much better proposition, for drainage is already provided and with the use of hypertufa they can be made to look like their stone counterparts.

Hypertufa is a mixture of sand, peat and cement which

is used to coat the outer walls of the sink to give it a natural stone-like appearance. It is easily applied by any home gardener.

Use a mixture of two parts peat, one part sand and one part cement. Mix this with water until the agglomeration is sufficiently stiff so that when a shovel is pushed repeatedly into it, the ridges that are produced remain in

The mixture should not be permitted to dry out too quickly or else it may crack and shale. If applied to the sink outside in the open it is wise to sprinkle the surface of the hypertufa periodically with clear water from a watering can with a fine rose attachment until it has firmly set. This may take a week or ten days.

In order to hasten the weathered appearance of the sink, mix together some animal manure and milk until it reaches a stiff consistency. Paint this on to the sides of the sink. There will be an immediate slight discolouration and within a few weeks a darkening and fine algal growth will develop giving a surprising look of maturity.

Sink and trough gardens benefit from being situated in a bright, open sunny position and placed so that surplus water drains away freely. Most gardeners find that raising their sinks off the ground on blocks or stones facilitates this, which coincidentally brings them to a better working height as well.

Ideally any sink or trough that is intended for planting should have provision for at least 6in/15cm depth of compost. Sometimes a deeper container that does not have adequate drainage can be successfully utilized if the extra depth is used for a generous layer of stones or gravel.

The compost that fills it must be free-draining. For most small growing alpine-type plants a soil-based

potting compost with a third volume of sharp grit added is adequate. However, bear in mind that commercial compost can be slightly alkaline and special provision will need to be made for lime-hating plants.

Any plants that have individual requirements can have a specific compost tailored to their needs, but with such a small container as a sink it would not be advisable to use more than one type of compost in an individual sink or trough.

Once the compost has been added, consideration should be given to the incorporation of small rocks. A standard sink can only accommodate a single rock, but troughs may be able to take two or three. This adds character to the feature.

Planting Troughs

A lpine plants are the most attractive proposition for sinks and troughs. Annuals and bulbs can be successfully accommodated, but using such containers for these plants is a lost opportunity.

When planting a sink with alpine or rock garden plants, provision should be made for colour and character at all seasons of the year, the plants being arranged as far as possible in a miniature landscape. By virtue of their restricted root-run most plants are likely to be temporary inhabitants, the majority of sinks and troughs demanding replanting and re-

character. If they collapse, the mixture is too wet; if they do not form properly and crumble, it is too dry. When satisfactorily mixed the hypertufa can be applied to the surface of the sink. To ensure that it adheres properly it is advisable to score the surface of the sink heavily and apply a coating of a waterproof adhesive (glue).

Stone troughs contain sempervivums; dense planting around them helps them to look comfortably settled.

As a sink or trough requires regular replanting, there is no reason to shun dwarf but not so slow-growing conifers if they are of attractive appearance. If these are carefully lifted when the replanting takes place and their roots are modestly pruned back they will form a neat, tight rootball, and, although not technically bonsai, will certainly retain their attractive character along with restrained growth and development.

Choose well-clothed varieties like the pyramidal *Chamaecyparis lawsoniana* 'Ellwoodii' with its fine blue-green foliage, or its golden form 'Ellwood's Gold'. *Juniperus communis* 'Compressa' is another lovely upright conifer of neat compact growth, while *Chamaecyparis lawsoniana* 'Minima' can be relied upon to make a tight ball.

Small-growing encrusted saxifrages like the grey-leafed, lemon-yellow flowered *Saxifraga aizoon* 'Lutea' are fine sink plants. So too the early spring-blossoming yellow *Draba aizoides*. This also makes neat bristly clumps of dark green foliage. The grey-foliaged *Raoulia australis* and many of the smaller primulas like 'Linda Pope' adapt readily to sink culture, along with the creeping *Hypericum reptans* with its golden saucer-like blossoms and the scrambling white flowered *Arenaria balearica*.

Creeping thymes are very useful for carpeting the surface of the sink, particularly in any small patches

arranging every three years or so.

The plants that can be successfully used are many and varied, but it is prudent to select only those that are of modest habit. A newly planted sink is always a delight, but if more boisterous plants like arabis and aubrieta are used, within twelve months it turns into an overgrown horror.

A dwarf conifer is always a useful investment, providing colour and character throughout the year. Some slow-growing conifers do not develop a pleasing habit until quite old and although they are theoretically ideal plants from the point of view of growth rate, they are not necessarily the most appealing.

where dwarf alpine bulbs are planted. Use them for tumbling over the edge to provide a softening effect. *Thymus serpyllum* and the varieties 'Pink Chintz' and the vivid red-flowered *T. s. coccineus* are amongst the most reliable and colourful, requiring little attention and living happily in a sink for many years.

Providing that sinks and troughs are kept in full sun and have adequate drainage they should be a success. Keep the use of fertilizer to a minimum, an occasional liquid feed during summer being adequate. Although a free-draining medium is vital, so too is regular watering, for sinks and troughs have a small volume of compost which is often subjected to baking sun. Regular summer watering is absolutely vital.

RIGHT: *The pedestal allows the conifer to cascade from its trough.*

BELOW: *Sink garden with dianthus and Penstemon pinifolius.*

POTS, URNS AND JARS

ABOVE: *Blue echeverias tone with their painted urn.*

OPPOSITE: *Large black pot of* Heuchera *'Palace Purple', positioned to play a part in a wall border.*

Choosing suitable pots and urns is a very personal pleasure. However, there are practical aspects to such selections which must influence decisions. It is of prime importance that the container is stable; also that it is spacious enough to take the amount of compost that its plant will require. The position of the container should also be carefully considered; different and even tricky sites are possible for, in addition to the normal free-standing pot or urn, there are now adaptations that can be used in awkward corners. Called corner-planters or quarter-circle bowls, they fit snugly into any right-angled setting.

For simple displays of summer-flowering pelargoniums or fuchsias in single plantings, a plain pot or urn is desirable. Perhaps a rope or rope-and-medallion decoration around the side might look engaging, but nothing as elaborate as a Florentine vase. This kind of urn with its classical but busy decoration is best suited to providing a home for a single clipped box or bay tree.

Planters with simple pattern markings, such as those popularly referred to as Greek carvings, look well when planted with herbs and scented plants. Soft fragrance and pastel shades add a Mediterranean feel to them.

Garlanded pots and urns have similar associations. These each have a sculptured garland in a single row which embraces the pot and are capable of taking more brightly coloured plant arrangements.

Bell pots, as their name suggests, are the shape of a bell, but upturned on a flat bottom. Sometimes they have a very simple pattern around the side in narrow discreet bands. Bell pots are amongst the best containers for plants as they are very stable and have the capacity to hold a generous amount of compost. While there is no reason why a display of bulbs or bedding should not be grown in such a planter, their configuration is much better suited to a permanent shrubby planting.

Camellias look especially fine in a bell pot.

Urns, irrespective of the materials from which they are made, are ideal for trailing and short-growing plants. They are not in harmony with shrubby plants, particularly narrow-waisted fleur-de-lys urns. These have wide rims over which it is customary to allow plants to tumble and a deeper central area in which more upright subjects are grown. Popular plants for urns include small leafed ivies, helichrysum and trailing nepeta, with focal plantings of fuchsia, pelargonium or cordyline.

When planting urns, remember that in many cases they are viewed from below, so the planting arrangement

25

Elegant urn suitably planted with a spraying cordyline.

Not all pots are of conventional shape: there are those that our forebears designed for specific plants and to which the name has remained attached. Strawberry pots can still grow strawberries, but those made of clay are more usually planted with choice alpines or herbs. The warm brown clay strawberry pot, with its planting pockets all around the sides, provides excellent conditions for sun-loving herb plants when filled with a gritty free-draining compost.

Crocus pots are similar, but have smaller round holes through which individual corms were planted. Many reproductions of Victorian crocus pots are now around, but they are mostly made from plastic and only suitable for indoor use. The old clay pots are excellent outside, especially the taller or more rounded versions. While these should be given protection during severe freezing weather, they can spend most of the year outside. Apart from crocus, try growing scilla, puschkinia or tiny daffodils like *Narcissus minimus* in them, followed in summer by South African ixia or sparaxis.

Wall pots are an acquired taste, but many gardeners with a very confined space find them invaluable. Their restricted rooting space, together with the reflective warmth of the wall upon which they are fixed and the general all round dry climate tends to limit the opportunities for growing interesting

should take this into account. Bold upright plants are not suitable, unless of strictly architectural quality, the spiky leafed cordylines appearing equally appealing from every viewpoint.

Some urns are squat and unwaisted, especially the old fashioned lead and reproduction sorts. These are planted more like tubs, although the plant associations must be quieter than perhaps considered appropriate for a white or light stone-coloured container. Soft fern foliage, along with ivy and delicate-flowered plants like the blue or yellow brachycome or purple-blue scaevola are most appropriate.

plants unless there is great commitment to watering and manicuring.

The only plants that unreservedly tolerate such indignities are ivy-leafed pelargoniums, sedums and sempervivums, along with petunias and one or two of the herbs. However, with careful placing and maintenance it is possible to raise many other combinations where care is of the highest order.

Some wall pots are of conventional rounded shape with holes in the rims by which they can be fixed by wires to hooks on a wall. These always look ungainly in their plain form, even when planted. A more pleasing effect is created by a little extra expenditure on a fancier kind with a pie crust rim. Such pots have a traditional charm and quality impossible to achieve with a common clay casting.

Half pots in which one side rests flush with the wall are easier to plant so that they appear to be an integral part of the wall rather than an appendage. Few have sufficient room to take more than one or two trailing plants, so for the best effect they should be grouped together.

Oriental pots and planters are attractive additions to the garden, adding colour and patterns to patio or terrace, but if not carefully chosen detracting from the planting. Most follow a theme that to a greater or lesser extent should be reflected in the surroundings.

Chinese dragon planters

Chinese pot with variegated agave is given its own trellis house as an architectural definition.

provide one of the more diverse offerings of present day potters. A few are of traditional designs, but many of the more pleasing works are a westernized view of Chinese art. Sometimes they are etched into the clay, other times painted in the glaze, but each needs a very tasteful planting if it is to retain

its charm, dwarf bamboo or broad-leafed aroids producing the finest contrast.

Malay-style pots, although finely painted, do not need such quiet planting. With their softer hues they can easily take brightly coloured flowers, providing that only one colour is used in each planter.

Hay boxes, lined with plastic and planted with daffodils and hyacinths, are used as an alternative to conventional boxes.

WINDOW BOXES

Window boxes come in all shapes and sizes, but most are of very restricted root-run. This needs to be borne in mind when selecting plants, for some of the subjects that will grow well in deeper tubs and urns would find life intolerable in a window box.

A lightweight compost is desirable for most window boxes so that undue strain is not placed upon the wall fixing, and while a soil-based compost is desirable it is not always as practical as the lighter weight soil-less types.

The latter used in such a small area as a window box means that nothing can live permanently in this position without being subjected to regular replanting. Thus the window box has become the home of transient annual plants and bulbs.

Spring

The spring window box is probably the most welcome. On a cold day a foretaste of the joys to come is just the other side of the window. If the modern universal strains of pansies are used, the window box can be colourful from mid-winter until the summer bedding plants take over. Until recently these lovely pansies

were only available as a mixed strain, but now they can be obtained in separate colours.

Polyanthus make a very cheerful spring display. Standard mixed strains like the Pacific Giants are well suited to window boxes, although for something special try the Cowichan Strain. Unlike the popular polyanthus varieties, this has flowers without central zoning. Each blossom is a solid colour.

Polyanthus mix easily with bulbous plants, especially the shorter-growing narcissus. Varieties of the cyclamen-flowered narcissus, *Narcissus cyclamineus*, such as 'March Sunshine' and 'February Gold' are excellent companions. These come into flower just before the

Window box with daffodils (including Narcissus *'Jumblie') and* Iris reticulata *'Harmony'.*

polyanthus, the latter hiding their fading foliage.

Early flowering squills like pale blue *Scilla tubergeniana* also provide very early colour. Indeed, these can often be associated with winter-flowering heaths like *Erica carnea* 'Pink Spangles' or 'Springwood White'. It is these heaths which provide much of the colour for the winter window box. Although all are designated as winter-flowering, it is quite possible to select varieties that flower as early as autumn and as late as spring. During the dead of winter, though, restrained but free-flowering varieties like 'Ruby Glow' are perfect for window box cultivation.

There is no need to depend upon flowers for colour either, for there are many golden-foliaged heaths and heathers, like 'Robert Chapman' and 'Gold Haze' which yield rich winter hues that provide a perfect foil for companion plants or winter-flowering bulbs such as the dwarf *Iris reticulata* varieties 'Harmony' and 'Joyce'. These are excellent bulbs for lifting the winter blues as they produce high quality blossoms the first season. This is where snowdrops and winter aconites fail for window-box culture. They need two or three years to become well established before giving of their best. Within the confines of a window box this is not possible and so regrettably they are best omitted.

ABOVE: *Fuchsia, argyranthemum and lobelia completely cover their box.*
RIGHT: *Window box used for a balcony; the plants include petunia, begonia and nemesia.*

Summer

While the winter and spring displays are greatly appreciated, it is during the summer that the gardener with a window box has the greatest opportunity to display his skills. A little time can be gained by pre-planting summer bedding, for nothing looks worse than a sparsely populated box during early summer. Most window boxes have inner containers, so it is quite easy to have each succeeding display prepared. By using linings it also means that, if you have had a spring display of bulbs, these can be allowed to die down naturally and without disturbance before being planted out in the garden.

Fortunately most of our summer-flowering annuals and bedding plants are easy-going and co-exist quite happily with one another. However, to create the best quality display a window box should only contain one type of plant. This means that the compost can be prepared for that plant's specific requirement and the subsequent watering and maintenance regime tailored exactly to its needs.

Pelargoniums, for example, enjoy full uninterrupted sunshine in a free-draining compost which is not too rich. If there is a high level of plant foods, especially nitrogen, then the plants will produce foliage at the expense of flowers. A lean hungry compost in a hot location will ensure a colourful summer-long spectacle.

Busy Lizzies (impatiens) prefer a partially shaded location and a compost that has a high proportion of organic matter. Recent research has indicated that busy lizzies prefer a compost containing a composted pulverized bark, a constituent which pelargoniums would abhor. So one can readily appreciate that a window box in which pelargoniums and impatiens are mixed is only going to meet with moderate success.

French marigolds, dwarf antirrhinums, lobelia and white alyssum are all more amenable to being grown together. For the best effect choose F1 hybrids. These have great uniformity of habit and consistency of flowering.

In preference choose those varieties that have been given awards by the Fleuroselect seed organisation. These are always designated in catalogues and the distinctive logo often accompanies bedding plants when they are offered for sale.

Tuberous-rooted begonias make a cheerful, long-lasting summer display for a window box. Both the upright growing and pendulous varieties can be grown, but the really large-flowered sorts are not suitable. Choose standard commercial strains which are usually sold by colour. To ensure a heavy crop of double blossoms, constantly remove the small single female flowers. These are easily recognized in the bud stage as there is an immature three-cornered seed pod behind each flower.

Fibrous-rooted begonias are another good choice, but do not mix these with double-flowered tuberous kinds. These are the small-flowered begonias that flower from early summer into the autumn, only succumbing to the first sharp frost. They are available in colours that range from white through various pinks to deep red and have glossy foliage that is either bright green or deep bronze.

UNUSUAL CONTAINERS

A nything that is capable of holding sufficient compost which will sustain plants is fair game for planting.

A popular and very successful receptacle is the old wooden wheelbarrow. Filled with good quality compost a barrow can become home to almost any combination of planting imaginable. It is important that there should be some pendulous material around the sides like the blue hanging-basket lobelia or perhaps the blue starry flowered brachycome, together with some leafy plants to provide solidity, but otherwise it can be a free-for-all. While there are innumerable varieties to choose from, lovelies-bleeding (*Amaranthus caudatus*) in both its purplered and green-flowered form makes an excellent centrepiece around which an informal display can be created. Informal it must be, for a formal planting in a wheelbarrow is a visual disaster.

So too is a cistern. Old cisterns are lovely planters, especially when placed with their backs to a wall, but once again their planting arrangement must be informal. Plant a cistern which is being viewed from one side rather like a flower arrangement with taller plants to the back. Bold rear plantings of clarkia with a tangle of pastel-coloured candytuft and 'String of Pearls' mixed lobelia in the

ABOVE: *Old lead cistern with an elegant assembly of pelargoniums, the succulent* Senecio kleinia *and young purple-leafed* Cotinus coggygria *'Foliis Purpureis'.*

OPPOSITE: *Antique wheelbarrow with a pouffe of* Argyranthemum frutescens, *pelargoniums and lobelia.*

foreground create a picture of subtle beauty which can be replaced in the spring with pink tulips and a frothy mass of azure-blue forget-me-not.

Modern glazed cisterns do not lend themselves readily to planting. Unless treated with hypertufa they are stark and ugly. Not so lavatory pans, at least not in some gardeners' eyes, for a pastel-coloured pan with brightly coloured pelargoniums tumbling over it is very much within modern-garden thinking, although for many it will for ever be an unsavoury novelty.

Chimney pots are now collector's items, especially the very tall ornate kinds, and so are becoming quite expensive. For colourful planting a plain pot is fine, even the

modern style of reddish-brown chimney pots can be planted very successfully with pink or red pelargoniums. The taller old-fashioned ones give a little more scope, but as they are very narrow, watering needs careful attention.

If you can gather a number of pots of different sizes and group them together a very attractive arrangement can be made; this makes what the Dutch like to call a mobile garden, where the floral show can be shuffled around at will to create the most pleasing picture. Most plants respond well to chimney-pot life. All kinds of pelargoniums, foliage varieties of helichrysum, petunias, verbena and brachycome grow particularly well.

The window is framed by the unbroken drapery of plants; those in hanging baskets and boxes link up with climbers grown in the ground.

HANGING BASKETS

Recent years have seen great changes to hanging baskets, affecting not just the diversity of styles that are now available, but also the plants which can be used. Modern pelargonium varieties that can be raised from seed are extremely useful, as are the latest Busy Lizzie varieties. Trailing lobelias are improving all the time and the grey and variegated helichrysums are now universally available.

Despite all these advances, the maintenance of a hanging basket demands as much care as ever before. As it is always

difficult to maintain moisture because of the constant drying effects of the wind, it is wise to add a little perlite to the compost. This is a white granular material derived from a volcanic rock which is capable of absorbing moisture and allowing it to be released back into the compost in drier periods. Up to a quarter by volume of perlite can be added to good effect.

Modern hanging pots are made of plastic and are not given to rapid drying-out. Culturally excellent, they are mostly aesthetically poor and not comparable with the

traditional wire basket with its lining of green sphagnum moss. Traditional baskets lined with moss are not as difficult to establish as one might imagine. The moss layer is built up gradually as the compost is added.

Trailing plants are pushed through the sides of the basket, the roots making firm contact with the compost and the moss tucked neatly around them. The building of the basket continues on upwards. When filled with compost, remove the pot from the plant that is to form the centre-piece. Place this in the middle of the basket and then plant all around it. The pot can then be removed and the pot ball of the centre-piece dropped into the waiting hole. This makes

RIGHT: *a dual hanging basket is ideal when a vertical feature is desirable on a house.*

RIGHT: *a dual hanging basket is ideal when a vertical feature is desirable on a house.*

filling the basket simple and ensures an even distribution of plants.

One needs to pay careful attention to the watering of a newly planted basket or hanging pot. If a watering-can is used the water will often flow irregularly through an open-sided basket. It is always better with these to soak them in a deep bowl until the compost has settled, taking care to avoid damaging any trailing shoots. A watering-can may be used subsequently providing that a fine rose attachment is employed.

The correct watering of hanging baskets is as important as the correct compost. It is vital that they are thoroughly soaked regularly rather than constantly sprinkled with water. If good drainage has been provided surplus water will quickly run away.

Occasionally a basket will dry out. Providing that the plants have only flagged and not shrivelled, it will not be beyond redemption. As the compost that is used for hanging baskets is almost inevitably of a soil-less kind and consists largely of peat, it is often difficult to wet again. The water will run around in globules on the surface of the compost and not penetrate the growing medium. If a small quantity of dishwashing liquid is added to the water it will soak through as if by magic. This only works with soil-less composts, having little effect on the soil-based kinds, but is an invaluable aid to survival when drying-out is a problem.

Planting Hanging Baskets

The choice of plants for growing in hanging baskets is legion and continues to expand each year. All kinds of plants that were rarely heard of previously have come to the fore in recent times. Plug production, the modern and very economical method of raising bedding and basket plants in tiny compost modules, has revolutionized the range of available plants as growers have searched for new varieties which adapt to this

LEFT: *Plants cascade to such depth that they double the length of the basket.*

OPPOSITE: *This colour-themed planting can be raised from one seed packet and includes alyssum, cerastium, lobelia, petunia and pansies (by courtesy of Thompson and Morgan).*

patiens are all candidates for such treatment. Not only do they have specialized compost requirements, but grow better in different locations. A basket of ivy-leafed pelargoniums will thoroughly enjoy a hot sunny corner in a free-draining gritty compost, while impatiens would grow better in a compost with plenty of pulverized bark added in a shadowy spot.

Single plant baskets provide great opportunities for colour theming. For years gardeners have aspired to produce blue or white or pink borders, but it is only very recently that themed baskets have been introduced. Modern strains of pelargoniums like 'Mini-Cascade' are perfect for such plantings, making huge balls of lovely colour. If single-colour fuchsia varieties are chosen, an equally beautiful effect can be achieved. The elegant 'Red Spider' and pure white 'Annabel' are two pendulous varieties that can be unreservedly recommended.

Pendulous begonias can be used in the same way. It is amongst these that the greatest choice of colourful basket plants can be found, ranging from pure white, through yellow and pink to deep fiery red. There are few

intensive method of culture.

For traditional baskets gardeners still adhere to the combinations of pendulous fuchsias, ivy-leafed pelargoniums, trailing lobelia, dwarf French marigolds and petunias. There is nothing wrong with this at all, for long-lasting and reliable colour is assured in a basket that is well clothed with foliage. When carefully considered though, it is quite remarkable that pelargoniums and fuchsias prosper together, for each has a very different range of requirements if it is to fulfil its potential. Grown together the result is inevitably a compromise.

This suggests that we should pay more attention to single plant baskets. Pelargoniums, fuchsias and im-

named varieties about, most being sold by colour. For either an intensely colourful show or a subtle pastel presence, pendulous be-gonias are dependable.

Hanging carnations are another reliable option. Colourful characters, these are often richly fragrant too. Although they require a very free-draining medium, they do not like to dry out, so very careful placing is called for. Popularly known as Tyrolean carnations, they can also be used for window boxes, combinations of baskets and boxes being evocative of the Austrian Tyrol.

Despite the obvious ben-efits of using a single plant in a basket, mixed plantings should not be neglected. For gardens of a less formal style they are perfect. While tra-ditional mixtures still hold court in some circumstances, the adventurous gardener should try his luck with some of the latest varieties. Apart from the lovely blue brachy-come, recent introductions have included the yellow-flowered bidens, variegated felicia and bright blue or violet scaevola, all beautiful plants that greatly enrich the garden.

37

HANGING PLANTS

In order to succeed with hanging baskets, or any pots that need to be concealed, it is essential to have a generous planting of truly pendulous plants. Sometimes, as with fuchsias, the container can consist entirely of a single variety. In fact few hanging baskets are more beautiful than those filled with a single fuchsia or pelargonium variety. These are successful not only because of the uniformity of growth and colour, but also because of the opportunity for providing exactly the right soil conditions for the plants. Pendulous fuchsias have very different requirements from hanging pelargoniums. This fastidiousness is not universal, however, and many other hanging subjects mix very happily with all manner of other plants.

There are many varieties of pendulous fuchsias, but the carmine and white 'Cascade' is amongst the most popular. This and other hanging kinds are easily grown both in baskets and containers, although in the latter they should be confined to the edge. In order to remain neat, compact and full of flower they demand regular manicuring, any stray shoots being pinched back to a leaf joint.

Hanging pelargoniums do not stray so much. These are best used alone, but traditionally have been part of a mixed hanging basket. The modern F1 hybrids are uniform, very free-flowering and of somewhat garish colours, the majority being ill-at-ease in a mixed planting. For maximum impact these should be used alone. It is older varieties like the pink-flowered, variegated-leafed 'L'Elégante' that are most satisfactorily accommodated in a mixed display.

The helichrysums have become very popular in recent years. Formerly known only as everlasting flowers, there is now a whole race of trailing foliage varieties that have descended upon us which bear no resemblance to our original conception of helichrysums. All are perennial, although not reliably so unless given protection, and easily overwintered with the minimum of heat. Predomi-

This container of the ivy-leafed Pelargonium 'Yale' stands on upturned pots to allow the plant extra space.

Tiny-leafed ivy spills onto the ground. It is partnered with the beautiful tender echeverias.

nantly plants for hanging baskets, they are also very good for window-box planting.

Helichrysum petiolare is the most widely grown, a stiff but agreeable tumbling plant with rounded grey felty foliage. A perfect companion for bright red or pink pelargoniums especially in a window box. It has a variegated cousin known as 'Variegata' and a soft sulphurous-green leafed variety called 'Limelight'. Each can be put to a wide range of tasks, living happily alongside most other popular summer plants in an open position, providing the compost does not become too wet.

In such circumstances ivies are more suitable. If the compost is likely to be very wet or ill-drained in a container, whether the planting be permanent or temporary, ivies are the most suitable candidates. Most *Hedera helix* varieties will tolerate such vagaries along with poor light conditions. The variegated-leafed kinds like 'Anne Marie' are very reliable; so is the crinkle-leafed 'Green Ripple' and arrow-shaped 'Sagittifolia', the latter two being particularly useful in traditional settings especially where the container has a Victorian flavour.

Lovely and simple hardy-annual planting of Specularia speculum.

HARDY ANNUALS

Hardy seed-raised annuals have a big part to play in container gardening. Not only are they the most economical way of growing plants, but they produce form and habit not easily found in other subjects. Their one limitation is an almost universal dislike of being transplanted, so special precautions are necessary to achieve the desired result. Few gardeners can have the luxury of sowing the seed directly into compost in the planter and then waiting for it to grow, for the period from sowing to looking respectable is going to be measured in weeks.

Use modular trays or small peat pots and sow annuals sparingly into these, thinning the young plants out

40

once they develop their first rough seed leaves. It is desirable to leave large-leafed annuals like the English pot marigold or calendula as individuals, but smaller plants such as linaria can be allowed to crowd together providing their development is not likely to be impaired.

The dwarf hardy annuals are very welcome, especially the fragrant night-scented stock. While not the most beautiful of plants, it must surely be one of the sweetest-smelling and can best be enjoyed close to a sitting-area. As this is also likely to be a visually important place, mix the night-scented stock with other more startling plants. It can be planted around a standard fuchsia in a tub without diminishing the fuchsia's impact, providing evening fragrance that no fuchsia could match. It is also tolerant of the damper soil conditions that the fuchsia enjoys.

Virginian stocks are cheerful pink-flowered annuals of diminutive stature but tremendous enthusiasm. These can be grown in almost any situation in the sun, being especially useful in a window box where their lovely tiny satiny blossoms can be enjoyed at close quarters.

The poached-egg plant, *Limnanthes douglasii*, is a must for sunny positions. It is a sprawling plant with white and yellow flowers which associate so well with its common name. These are produced all summer long and are ideal for a single colour planting. They are too

Splendid trough of foliage plants (begonias and fern) includes the hardy annual hare's tail grass, Lagurus ovatus.

startling to mix with most other annuals, but in a trough or window box where they can be grown alone they make a most satisfactory display.

Linaria is lovely for a cottage garden theme. These colourful little plants, which are popularly called toadflax, have spurred and pouched flowers, rather like an antirrhinum, amongst very fine and elegant foliage. Where informality is the key then these can be used freely, looking perfect in rustic settings such as hollowed-out logs, mellow stone troughs or

an old wheelbarrow.

Mignonette has a similar feel to toadflax, doubtless arising from its association with informal gardens of the turn of the century. Not a reliably hardy annual, but usually developing quickly from an outdoor sowing, it is the strange greenish-flowered plant that produces a haunting Victorian fragrance. If mixed with plants of the violet-flowered heliotrope called 'Marine' it is easy to create a container full of sweet-scented nostalgia.

RIGHT: Nasturtiums in a well-positioned pot on a cobbled path.

OPPOSITE: Simple elegant planting of eschscholzia in an old painted saucepan.

Plants for Hot Conditions

One of the greatest disadvantages of container gardening is the constant exposure of plants to hot sun. If the plants are to grow well they must have plenty of light; they are therefore put in a place where they can be enjoyed, and that is likely to be a heat-reflecting patio or terrace. So life can be very hostile for plants – which is where some of the hardy annuals can be useful. Amongst their number are several varieties that flourish under such apparent hardships.

The toughest are the nasturtiums, those wonderful brilliantly coloured bushy or trailing plants that look exotic, but in reality are amongst the easiest to grow. They are raised from large pea-like seeds which are merely pushed into the compost where you would like the plants to grow.

While nasturtiums flourish in hot spots, they do not relish exposure, so never be tempted to grow trailing varieties in a hanging basket: it will be a disaster. Dwarf kinds like 'Tom Thumb' are not much better, even their limited amount of leaf cover being very susceptible to wind. They are much better used in planters and can provide a startling show of colour if the compost is lean and hungry. A well fertilized compost yields masses of leaves and few blossoms.

For tub and window-box work the compact non-trailing 'Tom Thumb' is ideal, although the more sophisticated may prefer the variegated-foliage variety 'Alaska'. The trailing nasturtiums are much better for covering banks or climbing up trellis, but can be used to good effect in a tall planter on a pedestal or perhaps a planted chimney pot.

English or pot marigolds also enjoy the full sun. These are the bright orange or yellow varieties that were once the preserve of the herbalist. For informal arrangements 'Orange King' and 'Radio' are reliable old standbys, but for very formal plantings 'Orange Gitana' is ideal. This is a very short growing F1 hybrid that grows with almost mathematical precision and is a perfect plant for a window box.

Clarkia prospers in a sunny spot, but this rather rank and untidy annual with its bright red or lilac blossoms needs careful placing. It should not be exposed to wind as it tends to spoil, but in a hot sheltered place it will flourish. It is essentially a plant for the informal setting which looks particularly fine when planted in a container of mellow stone. In a small planter it can stand alone, but in a large setting it benefits from an association with taller plants such as the lovely pink spider-flower, *Cleome spinosa*. Plant a tub with a dozen cleome surrounded by clarkia and the effect will be charming.

Where both sun and wind are likely to create problems grow California poppy or eschscholzia. It is true that the wind may shatter some of their papery flowers of yellow and orange, but they are rapidly replaced and the plants will be undamaged. For hot, hostile conditions it is a must.

43

ABOVE: Nemesia umbonata *(above) with lobelia and verbena, set beside steps.*

OPPOSITE: *Plinth surmounted by potted pelargonium and lobelia. Valerian grows up to meet them.*

BEDDING PLANTS

Bedding plants make the most spectacular spring and summer splashes of colour. Of all the plants that are available to the home gardener, it is these that are the most versatile for display in planters and containers of all kinds. Spring bedding-plants include wallflowers, double daisies, forget-me-nots and other hardy plants, while summer varieties are mostly tender and have been raised under glass.

For summer colour the pelargoniums are difficult to beat, especially the modern varieties that are raised from seed. The two red-flowered Fleuroselect award-winning varieties 'Cherry Diamond' and 'Scarlet Diamond' are amongst the most free-flowering and have largely replaced the old-fashioned red bedding pelargonium 'Paul Crampel'. It is these which should be used in white planters, although along with subtle pink hybrids like 'May Rushbrook' and 'Princess Pink' they are lovely with terracotta.

'Simplicity' is a clear white-flowered pelargonium, while 'Grenadier' has brilliant red blossoms, but dark zoned leaves. For double-flowered varieties there are still only the vegetatively propagated kinds like the deep red 'Gustav Emich' and amongst the variegated-foliage pelargoniums the cutting-raised 'A Happy Thought' and 'Caroline Schmidt'.

Variegated and coloured-leafed pelargoniums make a lovely show in a plain, simple container. They do not associate well with fussy decoration and ornamentation. Some of the smaller kinds, like 'Golden Harry Hieover', adapt well to life in simple copper or iron pots or cauldrons. Be sure to provide a little drainage and water sparingly and they will make a delightful show.

Fuchsias on the other hand are better given more root-run. Although regarded as tropical plants they much prefer cool moist conditions and for that reason rarely produce their best results when planted together with pelargoniums. They also tolerate a little shade and providing it is not too gloomy can be used to lighten dull corners.

A number of the modern fuchsia varieties are too tall and vigorous to grow well in planters, but amongst the thousands that are available there are many suitable kinds for container cultivation, especially the dwarf varieties like 'Tom Thumb' and 'Lady Thumb'. Rarely growing taller than 9in/22.5cm, these are excellent for small planters and window boxes. So are the true bedding sorts like the strong red 'Dunrobin Bedder'.

Tubs and other larger planters can play host to stronger growing kinds such as the cerise and purple 'Dollar Princess' and 'Rose of Castile'. Only grow fuchsias in a planter in order to secure the best effect and plant sufficiently close to give complete foliage cover. This means that most modern varieties must be planted at 9in/22.5cm intervals. Large tubs will benefit from the use of at least two varieties; one for the centre and a tumbling type like the carmine and white-flowered 'Cascade' for the edges.

Consider foliage varieties as well: 'Cloth of Gold' has dark golden foliage and reddish leaf-stems while 'Genii' is almost a butter

Pelargonium, verbena and the yellow bidens; their pot is positioned to form part of a classic grouping.

yellow. There are small-leafed variegated-foliage varieties and a group of hybrids known as triphyllas. These have groups of slender orange-red or red flowers and foliage that varies from coppery-green to deep burnished bronze.

Seed-raised bedding plants have much to offer, especially the modern F1 hybrids. These are absolutely uniform in colour and character and for formal plantings are ideal. Most container plantings fall into this cat-egory, for tubs and boxes are usually arranged in a balanced fashion. It is only amongst the more unusual containers like chimney pots and wheelbarrows that the more variable open-pollinated varieties come into their own. For the most part these are components of the less formal garden.

Impatiens or Busy Lizzies are extremely useful because they will grow and flower well in gloomy corners. Providing you avoid the New Guinea hybrids, which are best treated as indoor plants, all the modern impatiens will provide a good show. As with pelargoniums they are best grown alone, for they like a damp moist root-run, preferably in a compost to which some composted bark has been added.

Begonias are a similar proposition, for they too enjoy a richly organic compost, but they are plants for a sunny spot. The free-flowering 'Non Stop' strain is wonderful, available in every colour imaginable, and flowers from early summer until the first autumn frost. Plant solidly in tubs, planters or window boxes for an easily maintained and reliable display.

Mixed plantings can be very successful if the right plant combinations are chosen. The first essential is that they should co-exist happily together, for amongst most bedding subjects there are opportunities to mix and match, such is the diversity now available. The key to successful combination planting is to use single contrasting varieties, not riotous mixtures.

In a spring display 'Primrose Lady' wallflowers surrounded by 'Blue Ball' forget-me-nots is startlingly beautiful in its simplicity and the same colour theme can be carried through into summer with 'Moonbeam' marigolds surrounded by 'Blue Mink' ageratum. It is often quite possible to repeat colour combinations from one season to the next, thereby giving the garden a continuity of character.

Bold contrasting plantings can also be important, especially in a confined area. Traditional bedding ideas can even be reproduced in tubs, such as red salvias surrounded by blue lobelia and white alyssum. To ensure that this is a long-lasting display choose one of the modern salvias like 'Volcano' or

'Rodeo' rather than the old-fashioned 'Blaze of Fire'. These have a much longer flowering period and are more uniform plants. Instead of edging with alyssum use 'White Lady' lobelia, planted with the dark blue 'Crystal Palace' or pale 'Cambridge Blue', which presents a much more professional picture.

In a cottage-garden setting a planter can be a brilliant mixture providing the plants all benefit from similar soil conditions. Zinnias, gazanias and Livingstone daisies are best omitted from any such scheme, but otherwise nemesia, annual pinks, French and African marigolds as well as asters and nicotiana can all be mixed happily.

The key to success with all bedding subjects, both summer and spring-flowering, is to feed regularly once flowering begins and keep on top of the dead-heading. Such simple regular maintenance ensures a long trouble-free show.

Begonia, gazania and argyranthemum with evergreen foliage behind as a foil.

ABOVE: *Daffodils and tulips set amongst wallflowers.*

RIGHT: *Choice arrangement of grape hyacinths (*Muscari azureum*) which form twin towers, held by an unobtrusive wire framework.*

BULBS AND TUBERS

*B*ulbous plants are amongst the most versatile for container cultivation. Indeed, such is their diversity that the gardener can find a variety to suit almost every situation imaginable. Whether as feature plants themselves or complementary highlights, they provide reliable colour.

When purchasing a bulb, the embryo flower is already formed inside, so that, providing conditions are not too difficult, a show the first season is virtually assured. The second and subsequent seasons may not be so good, for life in a planter, while perfectly acceptable up until flowering time, is not usually conducive to the production of quality bulbs for succeeding years. For this reason bulbs that have done service in a container are best planted out in the garden when they are over.

Spring

*P*ermanent plantings can be much enhanced by spring-flowering bulbs, especially those that the bulb grower refers to as miscellaneous bulbs. These include an exciting range of miniatures, including squills (scilla), glory of the snow (chionodoxa), aconites and snowdrops. All are marvellous complements to permanent plantings.

A scattering of snowdrops, especially the double-flowered

'Flore Pleno' around a tub containing a conifer provides a welcome breath of spring on a cold winter's day, in the same way that autumn-flowering crocus like *C. speciosus* enable us to cling on to the fading summer for another couple of weeks.

With permanent plantings of deciduous shrubs such as mollis azaleas use the bright blue squill, *Scilla siberica*. Its improved variety 'Spring Beauty' is exquisite. Chiono-doxa or glory-of-the-snow in its various guises is equally amenable, along with the very pale blue striped squill, *Puschkinia scilloides*. These reliable bulbs are amongst the few that can remain with a permanent planting and will come year after year.

The simple perfection of a grouped planting of the scented Lilium 'Olivia'.

Bulbs can also be used with bedding subjects, especially spring flowers like wallflowers and forget-me-nots. Both adapt well to life in a tub and benefit from the addition of single early or Darwin tulips. The opportunities for providing contrasting colour combinations amongst these groups of plants is enormous and is only limited by the gardener's imagination.

Tulips of one variety interplanted with either wallflowers or forget-me-nots of a single hue create the most attractive picture, but one which has an air of formality about it. In less formal situations choose the flouncing blossoms of the parrot tulips

to blend with old-fashioned mixed polyanthus.

In fact, spring can be made quite spectacular by the use of bulbs. Whether in single bold plantings or combinations the opportunities for the imaginative gardener are enormous. What is more, by the careful selection of varieties very accurate flowering periods can be achieved. While on the one hand this is very useful, it indicates that great care must be taken in bringing complementary varieties together. For example, not all blue hyacinths flower at the same time. Indeed, there can be as much as three weeks difference between two kinds, so the mixing and matching of varieties has to

be very carefully undertaken.

Hyacinths are amongst the nicest spring-flowering bulbs for tubs, providing not just beautiful waxy blossoms of great uniformity, but a rich and attractive fragrance. There are innumerable varieties to choose from in a wide range of colours, but the pure white 'Carnegie' and soft yellow 'City of Haarlem' are utterly reliable and flower at exactly the same time.

For single plantings the large trumpet daffodils make a bold show, but the named hybrids of the shorter growing and more elegant *Narcissus cyclamineus* are certainly worth considering. The bright yellow 'Peeping Tom' and silvery white

'Jenny' are charming and have a long period of blossom compared with many of their large counterparts. However, it is amongst the larger-flowered varieties that the greatest spectacle can be achieved.

'Spellbinder' with its sulphurous-yellow flowers is one of the finest for lightening up a gloomy corner, but we should not neglect old stagers like the bright yellow 'Carlton' and 'Golden Harvest' each of which have proved themselves over many years. 'Ice Follies' is one of the nicest whites and for those who are looking for an economically priced, but most attractive pink-flushed daffodil they could do worse than seek out 'Mrs R.O. Backhouse'.

Dwarf botanical tulips derived from *Tulipa greigii*, *T. kaufmanniana and T. fosteriana* are also excellent when grown alone. These flower much earlier than the bedding varieties of tulips, the common pinkish water-lily tulip, *T. kaufmanniana* being in full flower by early spring.

Pure white begonia and petunia with the violet scaevola.

Summer

*F*or the summer, cannas can take on the same role as tulips. While not technically bulbs, they have swollen rootstocks and are normally treated as such. Instead of interspersing them with other plants, make a bold central planting where their green or purplish-brown banana-like leaves can make a definite statement. Surround them with colourful short-growing bedding subjects like the modern named varieties of verbena.

Summer plantings are dominated by lilies. For many gardeners the cultivation of lilies in containers is the best way of achieving success with these exotic looking plants. Providing that the compost has extra peat or composted bark added to it, success should not be elusive.

The Mid-Century hybrids are some of the easiest and best suited to tub culture. 'Enchantment' is orange-red, 'Connecticut King', bright yellow and 'Destiny' soft lemon.

Also try the large-flowered white Easter lily, *Lilium longiflorum*, as well as the regal lily, *Lilium regale*, and the golden-rayed lily of Japan, *L. auratum*. When grown alone they are easily managed; cultural problems only occur when they are introduced to a mixed planting.

The same applies to tuberous begonias. These demand a free-draining compost with additional organic matter, conditions which most other summer flowering container plants do not enjoy. Grow alone, but perhaps with a centre-piece of a standard fuchsia, one of the few other summer plants that enjoy such a cool moist root run.

HERBS AND SCENTED PLANTS

Herbs are ideal plants for container cultivation. They adapt readily to the window box, planter or even hanging basket. Nothing looks finer than a hanging basket planted with parsley, making a big green leafy ball which can be sustained all summer if placed in a sheltered spot.

Planters and window boxes are slightly more conventional and work very well for those herbs popularly referred to as pot herbs. These are shorter-growing varieties of culinary herbs that adapt readily to pot culture. If they can withstand the constraints of a pot, then they should adapt easily to window boxes and planters.

All require a free-draining compost that is not too rich and an open sunny position. Pot-grown plants are readily available in the spring and it is better to start with these rather than attempt to raise your own from seed or cuttings. Although many herbs are perennial, when grown in containers they are best treated as annual and discarded each spring.

Most containers can be successfully utilized for herb growing, but one of the most appealing is the large terra-cotta strawberry pot. This has a place for a focal plant on the top and pockets around the side into which plants can be placed. Use a sage for the main plant, planting thyme, pot marjoram, and summer savory around the sides. Apart from being visually attractive, the plants can be readily manicured for culinary use.

While many gardeners grow herbs because they just like having them around, there are others who cultivate them for their culinary value. When this is the case place the container as close to the kitchen door as possible. Few cooks will wander far to gather herbs, so the closer to the kitchen the better.

Where decorative value is of at least equal importance then select finer forms of the herbs. Marjoram in its several guises is a green plant with purplish flowers much loved by bees, but it is a fairly mundane character compared with the golden-leafed form *Origanum vulgare* 'Aureum'. Although of greater beauty this is equally palatable.

So is the golden-leafed lemon thyme, *Thymus citriodorus* 'Aureus', and the variegated form of the common thyme known as 'Silver Posie'. Even parsley can be selected for its visual impact, the dark green crisp and curly variety 'Curlina' being amongst the finest and the one best suited to hanging basket culture.

On heavy clay soils, where most herbs find life impossible, containers can come to the rescue. Certainly rose-

Pots of herbs echo the circle at the centre of this wonderful enclosed formal herb garden which will retain both warmth and fragance.

mary, lavender and sage re-spond well to container culti-vation providing they are not permitted to freeze solid during the winter months. The same applies to bay, probably the most widely grown herb in tub culture. Not only can this be main-tained as a culinary delight, but clipped into balls, stan-dards or columns. The per-fect shrubby plant for high-lighting focal points in the garden.

Scented Flowers

While culinary herbs are a natural choice for a fragrant planting, there are many less utilitarian plants that can be used to great effect. Not only foliage plants, but those with scented blossoms too.

Pinks and carnations are some of the best, but they do not always enjoy a confined existence. They also require an alkaline soil if they are to flourish and so do not mix

easily with other plants. A free-draining compost is also required, preferably a soil-based potting compost which is not too rich. Catered for in this way and grown in terracotta they can be a delight, seemingly benefiting from the natural properties of the fired clay. They certainly rest comfortably in such planters while looking ill-at-ease in wooden tubs or any plastic contrivance.

In addition to well tried varieties like the white-flowered 'Mrs Sinkins', there are alpine pinks such as *Dianthus allwoodii* 'Alpinus' which are very compact and perfect for growing in a large strawberry pot. Do not overlook border carnations such as 'Tom' and 'Helen' or that most popular of dianthus the salmon-pink 'Doris'.

While summer-long fragrance can be offered by the pinks and carnations, spring depends upon bulbs, especially hyacinths. All hyacinths are richly fragrant and all will grow well in containers providing that you can accept the stiff formality of their blossoms. Reliable varieties include 'Pink Pearl', 'Delft Blue' and the pure white 'L'Innocence'.

Some of the narcissus are very fragrant too and window boxes provide the perfect place to grow the sweet-scented paperwhite narcissus. Nothing could be more lovely than their fragrant white blossoms on an early spring morning. Care needs to be taken that the bulbs do not freeze solid as this is one of the less hardy narcissus. It is

ABOVE: *Peppermint-scented-leafed* Pelargonium tomentosum *on the right.*

OPPOSITE: *Scented brugmansia (datura) and lilies in a small enclosed garden.*

always worth the risk though, the display being evocative of the spring to come.

Scented Leaves

Scented-foliage plants create less impact than those with fragrant flowers, for in most cases the aroma is not imparted until the leaves are brushed against or rubbed. However, those with fairly volatile oils can be encouraged to yield up their fragrance by being grown in a very sunny position. Warmth often permits the release of scent, especially amongst some of the lovely species pelargoniums.

Pelargonium tomentosum with its peppermint-scented leaves is one of the finest and

most attractive of this group, with handsome grey-green downy foliage. Often grown as a climber or wall plant, if it is regularly pinched back, the peppermint pelargonium can be turned into a dense, semi-scandent bush. The perfect plant for a large white urn.

The lemon and rose-scented pelargoniums are not so big and bold, but they can make an important contribution to mixed plantings, especially those where modern verbena varieties are being used. The pelargoniums have insignificant flowers which can be removed if necessary. This improves the foliage which is a lovely foil for verbenas, especially when they are planted in an old black pot or cauldron.

Even out of season, camellia foliage makes a shining back-cloth to the roses.

FOLIAGE PLANTS

opportunity of growing plants like phormiums or myrtle that may become damaged by late frosts or cold winds and which can therefore receive temporary protection. Also, gardeners on an alkaline soil can use the tub or planter as an opportunity to introduce a much-loved plant that cannot ordinarily be cultivated.

Evergreens

Bring these aspects together and one comes to camellias, that wide-ranging group of beautiful evergreens with brightly coloured, waxy spring flowers. For most gardeners camellias are essentially attractive foliage plants but which, with a little loving care, can provide a floral bounty too. Their dislike of lime can be countered with an acid-lover's compost and their susceptibility to late frost catered for by their mobility.

All camellias are fine foliage plants, but to ensure a bonus of spring floral colour choose free-flowering varieties like the deep pink 'Bow Bells' and 'St Ewe'. Both of these produce an abundance of blossom when quite young.

While it is rather nice to have the possibility of seasonal colour in addition to fine foliage the best foliage plants almost inevitably have the most mundane flowers. The myriad evergreen euonymus come into this category. This matters little, for amongst their number are some of the finest and most resilient evergreens

Permanent foliage plants are invaluable in the garden scene. They become doubly so when grown in containers, for you are then able to move them around to alter the perspective or add a new focal point. Some gardeners rearrange them as they might furniture, giving their garden a new outlook each year. Others take the

with variegated foliage. They come in all sizes too, from the dwarf-growing *Euonymus japonicus* 'Microphyllus' to the bold *E.j.* 'Macrophyllus'. *Euonymus japonicus* 'Ovatus Aureus' is the best of the golden variegated varieties, while amongst the silvery leafed kinds *E. fortunei* 'Silver Queen' is hard to beat. For plain glossy green leaves, *E. japonicus* 'Macrophyllus' is outstanding, a versatile plant that can be neatly trimmed too.

Deciduous Shrubs

Not all quality foliage need be evergreen, for amongst deciduous shrubs there are many handsome varieties that will respond to tub culture and still give of their best, especially if regularly stooled. This cultural trick works splendidly with many plants to yield high-quality foliage. It involves cutting them to the ground each spring, and as a result the shrub produces new vigorous young shoots with handsome foliage.

The purple or copper-leafed cotinus respond marvellously to this treatment, none better than *Cotinus* 'Royal Purple', with large rounded foliage of deep plum purple on strong wand-like stems. The golden elderberry, *Sambucus racemosa* 'Plumosa Aurea' is another fine candidate. It is a tough shrub that is usually quite ordinary, but when cut to the ground each spring, it throws up bold cane-like stems with

Inspired positioning whereby Aruncus dioicus *is a gleaming foil to the bronze phormium and golden bidens.*

enormous fringed golden leaves that give the draughtiest patio a touch of the tropical.

Clipped Evergreens

Clipped evergreens might be considered to be a completely separate aspect of container gardening with

little in common with tubs of riotous annuals. In visual and artistic terms this is certainly true, but the principles of cultivation are much the same. Good quality compost, a large container, together with regular feeding and watering are prerequisites for success. Add to this, the need for constant trimming and repotting every two or three years and one can readily appreciate that growing quality evergreens demands as intensive and skilled work as producing startling flower-filled tubs and hanging baskets.

There are many evergreens that can be used for tub culture, but for the majority of gardeners it is the various conifers which are most frequently grown. Those with needles like the spruce and firs do not adapt well to permanent tub culture, wit-ness the sad life of a Christmas tree continuously confined to a pot. For most needle-bearing conifers the constraints placed upon root development by the container, together with high summer soil temperatures, spell disaster. Not necessarily death, but certainly needle-drop.

The cypress-type conifers represented by chamaecyparis, thuja and juniperus are best for clipped evergreen work, along with the various kinds of yew, although the latter can be a bit tricky in tubs if placed in full sun. The easiest to accommodate are the varieties of *Chamaecyparis lawsoniana*. Not only do they adapt well to tub culture, but, as they have a tight habit of growth, they can be nicely clipped. There are several different foliage colours to choose from. The best green is 'Green Hedger' while 'Allumii' is blue, and 'Stardust' golden. Although rates of growth and habit are

Formal clipped box in a tub lapped by alchemilla and bergenia.

Neat conifers, Tsuga canadensis 'Jeddeloh', either side of a fountain of Carex pendula.

slightly different, with careful trimming there is no reason why uniform green, blue and gold pyramids should not be produced.

Amongst the broad-leafed evergreens, box (*Buxus sempervirens*) is a must. The original species can be clipped into any fanciful shape, be it a pyramid, ball or animal. Where pairs or groups of identical plants are required, grow 'Gold Tip'. This has splashes of gold on the tips of very handsome broad foliage which is strong and dense and produces a fine shrub for clipping. It is reproduced from cuttings and so every plant is alike providing it is given identical growing conditions.

For small shapes use *B.s.* 'Suffruticosa'. This is the variety mostly grown for edging in old gardens and can be trimmed to a very fine tolerance. Tradition has it that this variety can be reduced to the width of a box of matches without losing its foliage.

Apart from box the common bay tree (*Laurus nobilis*) is the most widely grown clipped evergreen. With a long tradition in topiary, trees that are either single or multiple balls of foliage are much prized, but, while easy to maintain do require winter protection. Bay survives most winters in a cool temperate climate, but with unclothed stems exposed to the weather, clipped shapes are much more vulnerable.

While balls and half-standards predominate, the bay is a very amenable plant and the imaginative gardener can come up with almost any shape. Whilst clipped bay is of limited value in the informal garden, where formality is the keynote it can make the garden, providing bold focal points and punctuation marks. In addition to the common green bay, there is also a lovely golden-foliaged variety.

CULTIVATION

ABOVE: *Witty box bird in its 'nest' (two pink eggs on the right?)*

OPPOSITE: *Even after rain, this urn of garnet petunias and Helichrysum petiolare 'Limelight' retains its beauty.*

Plants reflect in their growth the general condition and quality of the compost in which they are growing. For any kind of container cultivation to be a success the compost must be of the best quality. The use of soil directly from the garden, however well cultivated, cannot be unreservedly recommended.

Composts should be moisture-retentive, yet free-draining. In tubs, planters and window boxes they are best based upon a soil-based potting compost with at least one third by volume of sedge peat added. Hanging baskets are a different proposition, for they must be light in weight. Soil-less composts based upon peat, composted bark or coir are ideal.

The correct watering of containers and baskets is as important as the correct compost. It is vital that they are thoroughly soaked rather than constantly sprinkled with water. If good drainage has been provided surplus water will run away quickly and damping-off problems will not arise.

When only light watering is done the plants produce roots just beneath the soil surface. They are then vulnerable to hot sunshine and drying winds. Watering only sufficiently to darken the surface of the compost is not enough. The surplus must be seen running out of the drainage holes at the base.

Hanging baskets dry out much more quickly than tubs and window boxes. In some situations where they are exposed to full sun or constant drying breezes the plants will struggle. It is easier to identify these sites and avoid them, rather than fight a constant and often losing battle.

All containers and baskets restrict the root-run of plants to some extent and so regular feeding is essential. For sink and trough gardens this will be minimal, but for all other plantings the regular application of a fertilizer is essential. For summer-flowering annual and bedding plants this will need to be a quick-acting general liquid feed every couple of weeks, while more permanent shrubby plantings will benefit from an annual application of a slow release granular fertilizer.

The repotting of long-standing plants will need to be regular if they are to remain in prime condition, while plants of annual or shorter duration should receive fresh compost every time they are replanted. Likewise plants of all kinds benefit from a regular spraying regime. Use mutually compatible systemic fungicides and insecticides to provide on-going protection from common pests like greenfly and troublesome fungal diseases such as mildew.

With all plantings the removal of dead and drying blossoms and leaves is essential for continuity of flowering. Trailing plants need regular manicuring otherwise they become rank and unsightly. The regular pinching back of extension growths ensures that laterals are produced, which in turn yields bushier plants which give more cover.

INDEX

Philip Swindells has an international reputation in horticulture. Formerly Curator of Harlow Carr Gardens he is now principal of his own firm of international horticultural consultants. He has run workshops on specialist gardening and design topics, including courses on growing plants in pots and containers. His publications include seventeen gardening books and contributions to major horticultural encyclopaedias; he also broadcasts and writes columns for magazines and newspapers.

PRINTED IN BELGIUM BY

proost
INTERNATIONAL BOOK PRODUCTION

ISBN 1-55859-663-1